CHILDLIKE: THE PASSIONATE PU

LISA DOUGLASS

CHILDLIKE: THE PASSIONATE PURSUIT OF JESUS

LISA DOUGLASS

Published by Lisa Douglass

Rochester, NY

ISBN: [979-8-9919582-1-9]

Cover design by: Lisa Douglass

Interior design by: Lisa Douglass

Graphic Design, unless otherwise mentioned, created by the author using Canva.

Ballerina artwork, page 14, Keira Douglass

Giraffe Artwork, page 15, Lex Blaakman

For more information:

Lisadouglass.godaddysites.com

"If my heart could tell a story
If my life would sing a song
If I have a testimony
If I have anything at all
No one ever cared for me like Jesus
His faithful hand has held me all this way
And when I'm old and grey
And all my days are numbered on the earth
Let it be known in You alone
My joy was found"

-Steffany Gretzinger
"No One Ever Cared for Me Like Jesus"

LIVE TO

TITLE

THE HILT

TITLE

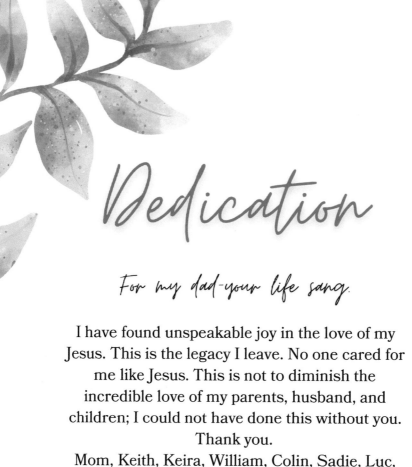

Dedication

For my dad-your life sang.

I have found unspeakable joy in the love of my Jesus. This is the legacy I leave. No one cared for me like Jesus. This is not to diminish the incredible love of my parents, husband, and children; I could not have done this without you. Thank you.

Mom, Keith, Keira, William, Colin, Sadie, Luc, Analise, Rowan, Penny, Judah, Oliviana, and Lia— it is in receiving your love that I have known and experienced God's love in real and tangible ways every day. Thank you.

Daddy, I miss you. Thank you for telling me my words were meant to be written.

Lisa D.

How to Read This Devotional

There Are Four Main Parts

The Story

The poems share memories from childhood and provide the context for the next two sections.

The Journey

In this section, I share my memories surrounding the poems so you can enter the world of the little girl journeying toward the heart of the Father. May this inspire your adventure deeper into the love of Father God.

Take Action

Lastly, you will be encouraged to participate. When you ask yourself the questions and take the time to make these lessons your own, you will see transformation. These are the little moments where your story is woven, and the fruit of investing time with the Creator will be beautiful. Let's journey together.

Prayer

I invite you to pray these words with me. The time you take to cultivate your own secret space of conversation with Jesus will transform your journey the most.

Prologue

Maybe the story should be in poetry?
The thought was unexpected.
My journals were full of verse and rhyme.

Interesting ...

Write it down.
Do you mean like a collection of thoughts written in
rhythm and everyday prose?

Journey.
The words roll like water on a leaf,
like a faucet that drips.

My Journey.

Interesting.

I did write it down.
From a ripe young age until my current day.
I have been writing, chronicling, living,
breathing, time away.
Could I possibly brave the light and crack the page?

My broken heart exposed and being healed.
Would I? Could I? Adventure called my name

It always does.

The Journey

I take Jesus seriously when He says we access His Kingdom through becoming like a little child (Matthew 18:3). His kingdom exists for the childlike. That blows my mind and fills my journals with the questions formed from that revelation. I love writing. I remember clearly the little desk that sat in my childhood room by the window. It overlooked our tiny street with rows of tiny houses and a constant stream of dog walkers and white-haired couples. Over the years, I created stacks and stacks of journals. I often wrote in three at once (a very confusing and frustrating habit if you like to read things in chronological order). I did not think I could tell this story. My recording of memories was so jumbled. But God invited me to remember. As the poem before beautifully describes, I sat there twirling my pencil, sitting at a desk that had grown too small for me, and committed to the process of healing.

It's time to dream again.

As a child, we are all told to dream big, and such exclamations are often accompanied by the fantastical stories of superheroes, underdogs, and creatures that talk. No one prepared me for the disappointment that follows when the weight of our humanity sets in and the possibility of fairy tales fades. Delightfully optimistic and daringly faithful, I threw my heart into the grandest of dreams—dreams spun from childish whims and seasoned with the unreachable standards of perfection and mixed with questions about the character of Jesus. These threads would tangle the tapestry of my story for years to come. Untangling would be my journey. This is an invitation to surrender to the process. Where false expectations and half-truths have shaped beliefs and defined maturity, Jesus says:

"Let the little children come to me."

Childlike is a journey to be known as created by Father God. Let this be your journey where you discover why and how you were created to be.

Take Action

"Let this be a sign among you, so that when your children ask later, saying, 'What do these stones mean to you?' then you shall say to them, 'Because the waters of the Jordan were cut off before the ark of the covenant of the LORD; when it crossed the Jordan, the waters of the Jordan were cut off.' So these stones shall become a memorial to the sons of Israel forever." —Joshua 4:6-7 NASB1995

Memorial stones are powerful. When hard times come, we need to remember the same God Who brought us through those troubled waters will settle us safely in the Promised Land. So get ready! You will need a journal for this book. The *Childlike Companion Journal* goes beautifully with this, but a regular composition notebook or an app on your phone works, too. Don't skip the journaling prompts.

Next, you will need to be honest. You can read this like a good story, but without your participation—that will be all you experience. If personal transformation is your goal, be UGLY honest. These will be just sweet stories unless we take action. Commit to the journey.

Whenever we commit to setting up memorial stones, we cultivate faith and faithfulness because we are setting ourselves up to remember the goodness of God in tough times—times when external reminders would be helpful. Do you have areas of your life that are painful to remember? Maybe they are tragic. Maybe you have been told those feelings don't matter. They do. Let's invite Jesus into this space.

Lastly, be *Loved*. Let Love walk into your room and show you Who He is, was, and always will be.

The Prayer

Note: You can pray and personalize as you like. These are not magic words. This is conversation with Jesus. Miracles happen as we bring our hearts believing God can and will heal.

Jesus, I feel afraid. There are parts of my heart I don't want open again. There are parts of my story I don't want to remember. Help me. Help me see what is needed to see and forget what I need to forget. Show me Love—the Person—in the places I am afraid. Amen.

I Want to Be a Giraffe

I want to be a giraffe.
The four-year-old version of
myself dons hand-me-down
tap shoes, too small,
but just right.

A giraffe that dances,
that is my dream.
A great-long neck.
Oh, the glory of being tall!
Smooth golden, glowing skin,
sunspots and all.

And as this four-year version of
me spins, time stands still or
maybe moves too fast.
I whisper over and over.

"I want to grow up and be a
giraffe,"

And as the words begin to swirl,
I think of Grandma, Mother,
Aunt.

I think of every child and adult I
have ever known in my long,
little life.

I stop spinning.

For a truly heartbreaking
moment,
I stare at the imaginary,
graceful creature of my
future in the face
and slowly–
like a sunrise,
this truth breaks through:
I cannot be you.

No child, nor adult, I ever in
my short, full life knew
Grew up to be a giraffe.
I sigh.
I contemplate.

I spin and kick off the too-tight
tap shoes.

I will be a ballerina.

And that is how my story
begins.

2

The Journey

"Now faith is the substance of things hoped for, the evidence of things not seen." (Heb. 11:1 NKJV)

"I would have lost heart, unless I had believed that I would see the goodness of the LORD in the land of the living." (Psalm 27:13 NKJV)

I honestly thought I could become a giraffe. At age four or five, I believed that's how animals came into being. I thought people just decided. Adults asked all the time, "What do you want to be when you grow up?" I figured some people chose to be animals.

Dancing ballet in too-small tap shoes is a real memory for me. It created a profound moment in my life because it was a moment of paradox. Children cannot become animals—that is a childish desire. But to dream of the impossible with hope—that is *childlike.*

It's important to distinguish between childish and childlike. There are immature, selfish, naïve, beliefs and behaviors that are *childish* because they detract from our ability to grow in life and relationships. If I were so dissatisfied with my present human self that I *still* thought the very best thing in life would be to become a giraffe, that would no longer be humorous, that would be a problem.

Maturity retains the beauty of being childlike—the persistence of pursuit and a beautiful innocence that is blind to the seemingly impossible—but follows those traits with actionable steps. The most delightful part of the memory is that I traded one dream for another, an almost equally innocent and unlikely dream: a ballerina in tap shoes. It reflects a heart posture of pursuit as we journey. We run committed to the Giver of our heart's desires, the Author and Finisher of our faith. That is *childlike.*

A proverb I love is, *"It is the glory of God to conceal a matter, but the glory of kings is to search out a matter."* (Proverbs 25:2 NKJV) We can delight in seeking because *He is near to all who call on Him. He is found by those who seek Him.* (Psalm 145:18 NKJV) He doesn't hide hard.

Faith and trust go hand in hand. There are seasons when God feels distant, so we pull out our memorial stones and remember that even when God hides, His children delight in seeking Him. It is not the frantic searching of a fearful, lost child. This search looks more like a tender pause that commits to finding God's dream—a dream that may look like becoming a ballerina.

God Dreams

As an adult, sometimes I have comforted my heart by saying, "In Heaven ... I will see, know, or understand XYZ." And while it is true that Heaven will be a place of amazing revelation and answers, now is the time for seeing. Now is where faith becomes substantial: "Now faith is the substance of things hoped for, the evidence of things not seen" (Hebrews 11:1 NKJV).

In the trials of life, with childlike tenacity, we hold on to the Giver of dreams and let go of the ideas that carried us for a season and. He has called you royalty—kings and queens—so search Him out. As you read, commit to going on an adventure with God. Like a little child taking His hand, delight in searching Him out. And don't be too quick to name your dreams childish. As for me, I am not dead. I may yet become a ballerina.

Take Action

Grab your journal. As an act of faith, write down one of the scriptures that caught your eye, a line you read, or a memory. Don't make it about logic—Let it be surprising. Just write down the phrase that is "sticking." Take that faith action. As you journey through this book, expect to find God. Like a parent who hides in plain sight, God is right here. Available and waiting.

Remind yourself of this next time you step outside or look out the window. Look for something small, a bit of nature. A blade of grass or a little stone. And ponder all the amazing things that needed to happen to get that little stone right at your feet. Like a little child as you walk to wherever you are going, take five minutes to accept the Creator's invitation to savor the art He leaves for us to discover. This journey is uniquely yours. Let's go adventuring.

"He has made everything beautiful and appropriate in its time. He has also planted eternity [a sense of divine purpose] in the human heart [a mysterious longing which nothing under the sun can satisfy, except God]—yet man cannot find out (comprehend, grasp) what God has done (His overall plan) from the beginning to the end."—Ecclesiastes 3:11 AMP

Prayer

Father, I invite You into my journey. Be with me as we go into this season. Show me Your love in a new way. Most of all, show me what it means to be childlike.
Amen.

Isaiah 40:28-31 NKJV

"But those who wait on the LORD
Shall renew *their* strength;
They shall mount up with wings like eagles,
They shall run and not be weary,
They shall walk and not faint."

Eagles Wings and Dreams

Child: Where is the plaque that was on the wall?

Mother: The plaque on the wall?

Child: Yes, the one with the verse about eagles' wings?

Mother: I have never seen a plaque on the wall.

Child: But Mother, yes you have! It has been there for a very long time. And just last night the moon was shining so bright, and I could not sleep, and I got up, and there it was. It is mine. It is my plaque. It is my verse. Where did you put it?

Mother: What did it say?

Child: You know, it was the verse about the eagles. God promised that I would run and not get tired. I am not very old yet, but I am not going to grow old, either. He promised.

Mother: Who promised?

Child: God, in the verse. Now, where did you put my plaque?

Mother: Darling, I have never seen that plaque. I do not think there has ever been one on the wall. But come, I will read you your verse.

The Journey

I was only a little older than during my "giraffe revelation" when another pivotal event happened. I woke up in the middle of the night (or at least I thought I was awake) to a room filled with the brightest moonlight. I shared a tiny room with my older sister, and I remember wondering how she could sleep through such bright light. Mesmerized by the beautiful moon rays and brilliant starlight, I tiptoed out of bed, my ever-gangly legs moving less than gracefully as I tripped over my nightgown.

It was then that a strange thing caught my eye. There was a tiny plaque on the wall that had a painting of an eagle with Isaiah 40:31 written on it. I had never seen it before. It was what I call a "granny plaque"—a little wooden decoupage and oil painting piece, something you would see in Grandma's kitchen. The other strange thing was that I knew what the words said, yet I'm not sure I could read them at that age. My heart filled with fire and excitement as the message burned into my soul. But most peculiar was the message my heart received—I could fly?!

What child does not long to fly? Here I was, with my very own promise that I would mount on iridescent wings and soar. While the revelation about giraffes assured me that I couldn't expect to sprout wings and become a bird, there was something in my childlike acceptance that God would show up with strength. That solidified a bedrock belief: Peace and hope from God would fill my life, and it would be *like flying*.

I woke up the next morning and searched for my special plaque, but there was nothing on the wall. My mom had no idea what I was talking about. She insisted she had never seen the plaque. I thought she was hiding the fact that she had secretly cleaned the room while I was sleeping.

The Journey

Although I was disappointed there was no plaque, I clung to the memory of that moment and to every mention of Isaiah 40:31 or reference to eagles that followed. The promise of mounting up on wings like eagles and not growing weary when we wait on the Lord became more than just words—it became a deep, personal truth. I never saw that plaque again, and the mystery remains unexplained, but the promise is forever burned in my heart.

Moments like these define us. They are the times when the divine intersects our everyday reality and invites us to believe that we are more than what we can see or touch. We can choose to hold on to these moments as memorial stones, or we can dismiss them as fleeting imaginings (or whatever excuse we offer ourselves). To become truly childlike requires faith—the kind of faith that holds fast to our dependency on the Father and embraces all that is closest to the Kingdom of Heaven.

Take Action

"The Lord answered her, 'Martha, my beloved Martha. Why are you upset and troubled, pulled away by all these many distractions? Mary has discovered the one thing most important by choosing to sit at my feet. She is undistracted, and I won't take this privilege from her.'"
Luke 10:41-42 TPT

Have you ever had something stuck in your head? Maybe it's a scripture or phrase that you just can't stop thinking about. Are you too busy to sit and savor that song that resonates in your heart, inviting you to explore healing? This is what it means to become childlike again—to delight in the subtle encounters of Heaven. Today, ask for eyes to see, savor, and hold on to the moments when Light walks into your room. Take a moment right now and wait. There doesn't need to be a dramatic show or sparkly lights for the moment to be significant. It doesn't even have to feel "right" or comfortable (See Luke 10:38-42).

Take a few minutes right now to put aside the noise and choose the "better part."

The Prayer

Father, You said that in order to enter Your kingdom—the place where You dwell —we are to become like children. Teach me what that means. Restore what was tangled in the tapestry of my childhood. Show me what You are really like.

I Don't Want to

I don't want to grow up,
Can I grow down instead?
I want to be small, really small.
I want to be loved, little, held.

I don't want to grow up and
do the things that grown-ups do.
I want to be small, really small.
I want to be loved, little, held.

I don't want to grow up,
Can I grow down, instead?
I want to be free, funny, loving.

What is worry, wonder, fear?
I don't want to grow up and
Move far from here.

Babies are born with bare feet.
Grown-ups wear shoes to guard
against spreading
Dirt, disease, and mud.
I make mud pies,
 Spaghetti from grass clippings,
   meatballs
and gutter sauce.

I collect worms.
I rescue birds.
I get lost playing Capture the Flag.
I take entirely too long to walk around
the block.

"Seeing what was happening, Jesus called for the parents, the children, and his disciples to come and listen to him. Then he told them, 'Never hinder a child from coming to me but let them all come, for God's kingdom belongs to them as much as it does to anyone else. These children demonstrate to you what faith is all about.' " Luke 18:16 TPT

GROW UP

Imagination games,
I love them.

Grown-ups travel to fill a page with pictures,
Grown-ups hardly see the airplanes rise,
the funny sparrow, the way the grass grows in spikey patches near the pool.

They only sigh and say, "You forgot to write, *'and.'* "

All the amazing things that fill my days, I never want to miss.

I don't want to grow up, but strangely,
Time won't stand still.

I remember that walk home from swim lessons. It was only a block and a half away, and I was 8 years old. My friend and I had strict instructions to walk straight home to our little house on the cul-de-sac, and we did. The only problem was that we walked slowly—really slowly. Completely lost in our imagination, we lost track of time, and my panicked mom drove around the neighborhood, envisioning the worst. It was an unfortunate coincidence that she went one way, and we came home the other. She found us almost home and grilled us with questions and rebukes—the fear evident in her voice.

I can still feel the childish resentment at being scolded for doing what she had told us to do. At the same time, my conscience bothered me because I knew we had been slow to obey. As a kid I think we all know when we are just making excuses. It was scary for us to dawdle, and I wasn't thinking about safety.

There was also something innocent in my desire; I just wanted to be able to play undistracted and unworried. I wanted to take my time and enjoy it. This tug of "childish" is centered on self—what *I* want, what *I* dream, or what I think. Being childlike is different. To be childlike is a gift, full of faith, hope, and love. Wonder is a gift. I want to get lost traveling roads I knew like the back of my hand. I want to discover the world that would blossom before our eyes if we would stop to see.

While childhood is where the longing to be *childlike* was born, childhood is also where the story is tangled with the vices of simply being *immature*. Adults worried about kidnappings, money, and the weather. I didn't want to worry, so I dragged my feet and ignored the danger. I longed to be a kid forever because I was afraid of growing up. Instead of pressing into childlike faith, trust, and wonder, I fell into the very "adult" trap of becoming afraid. I embraced fear and arranged my life to avoid the things I dreaded. But the problem was that what I was working so hard to sidestep was unavoidable. Everyone grows up.

Take Action

Read Luke 18:9-30. Ask God to speak to you through the passage. As you read, notice the different groups of people mentioned: Pharisees, tax collectors, children, and a rich young man. What differences do you see? How are they similar? Jesus welcomed all to His table. He is a safe place for the hungry.

Perhaps life has taught you that being vulnerable is dangerous. But God is asking, "Will you trust Me with your heart?" I was scared of being wrong and making mistakes, and in that fear, I became afraid to BE—to feel, learn, discover, be humble, and, most of all, be honest.

There is a childlike trust that is cultivated in being still in the middle of the exposure of our hearts. Read John 8:1-11. This is where a woman is caught in the act of adultery. In one of the most exposing scenes in the Gospel, she is then thrown at the feet of Jesus for judgement. She has no way out and according to the Law, she gets the death penalty. But Jesus bows low, challenges her *accusers,* and *redeems* this horrible moment in this woman's life with a message of hope.

When we open our hearts to be known by God we will never be met with condemnation. BE STILL. Listen for the voice of our Redeemer in the middle. When He speaks, He breathes the words of grace that empower us to walk another way.

The Prayer

Pray Psalm 139 with me:

1 You have searched me, LORD,
   and you know me.
2 You know when I sit and when I rise;
   you perceive my thoughts from afar.
3 You discern my going out and my lying down;
   you are familiar with all my ways.
4 Before a word is on my tongue
   you, LORD, know it completely.
5 You hem me in behind and before,
   and you lay your hand upon me.

6 Such knowledge is too wonderful for me,
   too lofty for me to attain. ...
13 For you created my inmost being.
   you knit me together in my mother's womb.
14 I praise you because I am fearfully and
   wonderfully made.
   Your works are wonderful,
   I know that full well. ...
23 Search me, God, and know my heart;
   test me and know my anxious thoughts.
24 See if there is any offensive way in me,
   and lead me in the way everlasting.

Psalm 139:1-6, 13,14, 23, 24 (NIV)

Invisible

Coping Habits

I slip into corners,

I fill large shadows.

I spill milk at every meal.

"Thank you for helping clean up, dear."

It is a handy trick to be invisible.

You don't have to say a word.

You can smile or frown.

Giggle

     ... or cry,

but only one tear.

Tears make you visible.

Feeling anything too strongly makes you visible.

So every day I go into my room,

and I imagine a very large rug.

I end the day with a very large broom,

big enough for very large feelings.

16

I lift the rug
And sweep.
I lift the rug
And sweep.

I sweep away
my awkwardness,
I sweep away the pain,

I sweep away
the hurt
of never really
feeling like
I have
a place.
I sweep it all away.
I turn my back
and it is invisible.
It
is all

Invisible

And I
cry
only
one tear.

The Journey

Some memories I wish were not true. There was an imaginary rug under which the teasing of my friends, the scolding of my parents, and the terrible loneliness I felt were all swept away. I chose to hide all my feelings, denying everything until I believed I was in a peaceful state of not experiencing strong emotions. However, sometimes when fierce or frightening emotions would surface, it meant trouble. Why did others seem to have "thicker skin"?

"You are too sensitive!" This common refrain slapped my already tender heart. There was no grace or compassion in my heart for the awkward girl trying to figure out her place. Instead, a skewed list of "facts" piled up in my mind and created an identity that Jesus was not speaking over me. Yes, I tended to be clumsy. I got blamed for spills, and deservedly so. I dropped things—a lot. I opened doors and would still run into them. With big glasses, curly hair, and definitely fitting into the "bigger-sized" category, I could have auditioned for every awkward-girl movie ... only I didn't magically transform when I shook my hair down and put on makeup.

Comparison ate away at my self-confidence, and as time went on, the God-sized dreams to be all God created for me shrank to my skewed perspective. I prayed to be anyone else but myself. I hated who I was. I wanted to escape the clumsy, giraffe-like body (all arms and legs and a big middle) I had longed for but now felt trapped in. I wanted to be more like my sister. She was, in my eyes, the highest standard of being—wildly popular, gorgeous, and always seeming to know what to do in social situations.

I had friends; I just felt ... out of place. To avoid criticism, I decided to simply not attract attention at all. I wanted to be unseen. Then the enemy whispered, "Be unnoticeable. Be unknowable. Be safe. Don't make waves. Just serve others. You don't need anyone." I believed the lies. Looking back, the lies are obvious, but at the time they seemed like humble, sweet, and even godly ambitions. Jesus was a servant with no reputation, but He did not reject community, confrontation, or vulnerability. The rug was my defense mechanism—my false savior.

The Journey

The tragedy is that the "safe, invisible Lisa" could live a relatively normal life. That version of myself was liked by adults and enjoyed by friends. Sure, deep relationships were difficult, and loneliness plagued my existence because I was terrified of being known. But I was in control of the access people had to my heart. Freedom from those fears would be a process that would take years, but it would also involve being willing to face the inadequacy and shame I was stuffing away.

Take Action

What events in your life stirred a sense of a need to protect yourself? Invite God into that place. Ask, "Where did I first learn I cannot trust people (and/or God) with this part of my heart?"

I loved hanging on monkey bars. I was quite good and could cross them with no problem, despite my larger build. I would pull myself up and do flips and tricks. One time, in my preteen years, while I was on the monkey bars, I got my pants caught on a screw and ended up with my underwear showing, stuck in a position of total awkwardness.

It made no rational sense, but in that moment, I believed I was super fat, destined to live my entire life embarrassed because of my size. To my knowledge, nothing was said about my size at that moment, but I embraced the *thought* that said, "If I were smaller, that embarrassing thing would not have happened to me." It was not true, but the thought took root. That was one of the feelings I swept under the rug. *I am not good enough.*

Healing comes when we invite God into the narrative of our past and allow Him to rewrite, comfort, and breathe life where darkness lies. Jesus was in the room, sitting by that rug, and crying the tears I wouldn't cry. He was outside on the playground. He wants me to see His face right now. Despite what I feel, He is still available with love at this very moment. My choice is to turn my face to look.

Take Action

Read Ephesians 1. I particularly like to read it in The Message translation, because the language is so open and relevant.

Do you have a memory that has defined you in a painful way? Have you invited Light to fill that space with truth? Sit for a minute and ask God to bring healing to that place. Journal about it. If you can, seek out a friend to pray with and speak the truth about that experience. Healing happens in community. Sometimes the best thing we can do is to sit at the feet of Jesus. So take a minute now. Release all the feelings of what you "should or could" do. Take a deep breath and listen.

Prayer

I'm going to pray a prayer based on The Message version of Ephesians 1 over you:

Father, I ask that You make each person who reads this intelligent and discerning in knowing You personally. May their eyes be focused and clear, allowing them to truly SEE who they are and what You are calling them to do. Help them to recognize themselves as the glorious inheritance that Christ went to the cross to preserve.
I speak strength over Your precious ones—endless energy and boundless strength in Christ Jesus. May they soar high on wings of faith, empowered by Your love.
Amen.

Sleep

I fall asleep in church.
I cannot keep my eyes awake.
It is as if some unseen force wills them closed,
and it is beyond my control. My eyelids fall and
I drift asleep.
Service ends and I am awake.
Oh, how I hope someone invites me to their
house to play.

The Journey

I remember trying so hard to stay awake during church services. We went to a little church where whole families did the service together. It was wonderful and challenging. Sometimes the sermons resonated with my child's brain, but most of the time, I struggled to stay awake. I couldn't wait for the sermon to be over so I could have fun with my friends.

I felt so guilty that I could not stay awake. I felt bored, disinterested, and so alone. Tangling the tapestry was also the growing desire to please those around me. I had no idea how to conceptualize the delight of the Father, let alone be satisfied by His approval.

As I grew up, I saw my older friends making mistakes, and I didn't want to make the same mistakes. I saw the pain that parents went through when kids "rebelled," and I didn't want to be "that kid." But I also didn't want help. Help made you needy. And to be needy meant I was seen, and if I was seen, then I was known. Ultimately the lie that was wedged inside was if I was known, I would not be loved because I was fat, awkward, tall, too honest, all wrong for this world.

Oh, what a tangled web we weave when we believe what was meant to deceive. Childhood is a vulnerable time. That vulnerability and trust make childlike faith so transformative in its simplicity. There are lessons we learn as children that shape our lives for good and beauty. At the same time, there are words and deeds spoken and done that threaten our journey and keep us locked in the past if not properly dealt with. For me, I felt lonely and out of place, which created a hunger for acceptance; this lack perpetuated the lie. What is your story? What did you miss in your childhood that has created longings still present today? Intent on restoring identity, God has a radical journey of healing ahead, in the light of a loving Father.

Take Action

Give yourself an hour or so to do this one. You won't regret it. One of the most powerful things we can do as we untangle childhood is recognize we need awakening. Children are not afraid to allow themselves to feel the unanswered need for more. That is the messy side of childlike-Children hope for more.

So my challenge to you is to hope again. Be willing to open up the box we have crammed our experiences into and lift the corners of the rug under which we have hidden hurts. Dare to believe that the "ugly", that has been called reality is simply not true. Dearest friend, we must be willing to go deeper and face pain. A power tool for demolishing lies that have become a part of our identity is writing something I call the Black Book. The Black Book is where you write down the negative thoughts running through your head without any censoring. Do not excuse or be in a hurry to explain how you know such-and-such a thought is not true. Just write. This is not about you fixing anything or proving anything. This is a simple act of surrender and encounter.

Example:
First: Write It Down (BE HONEST). The lie I believe is: "I am a bad mom."
Second: Confess: This is a lie, and believing this separates me from God (sin).
Third: Flip the Script. Ask powerful questions. *Jesus, What do You say about me?*
Fourth: Listen. Don't rush or overthink this step. God speaks, and He will gently lead you.
Fifth: Be Filled. Let Jesus' voice replace the words of accusation and inadequacy. As you sit in the quiet, write down the words, scriptures, or pictures that come to mind.
Lastly, Declare: Make those thoughts a prayer, confession, and a new standard. Don't allow those old accusations to linger. When lies creep in with baggage that looks like justification, remember that the blood of Jesus has spoken a better word, and declare the Truth.

The Prayer

I have been bought with a price; I am a new creation. I am Your beloved, and You are mine. I am who You say I am. I am chosen, accepted, and loved. I am not alone. You are enough. Jesus died to pay for all my inadequacy. I am complete in Christ. You have good plans for my life. You are a refuge—a safe place. I rest in You. Amen.

Who Are You

Holy

Lowly worm am I

High and lofty King,

I mean no disrespect.

Please hold Your lightning and let me ask,

Are You an angry Santa?

A godly, goodly man,

Are You waiting for creation to be good?

I hear my parents talk about You.

Like people lost in a desert,

they thirst for You.

You fill their

thoughts and conversation.

And all the while I wonder–

Who are You?

Maybe if I didn't fall asleep in church ...

The Journey

One of the most powerful modes of transformation comes when we dare to ask questions. Have you ever wandered through a carnival filled with those whimsical mirrors that distort your reflection, making you look too tall or too short? Memories can act like those funhouse mirrors, bending and twisting our perceptions of reality. If we lack a paradigm that gently questions the reflections we see, we risk crafting faulty conclusions about life and ourselves. I, too, found myself caught in these tangled beliefs.

As children, we absorb enchanting stories about figures like the Easter Bunny and Santa Claus, eagerly awaiting gifts that promise to rain down upon us ... if we are good. This notion—that if we're "good enough," blessings will shower us—is a comforting yet misleading idea, woven deeply into the fabric of our culture, religion, and hearts. While I understand the impulse to encourage good behavior in little ones with the allure of toys and treats, I also recognize how such conditioning can birth unhealthy beliefs that linger, often unnoticed, for years.

I never truly believed in Santa, though I longed to. I even climbed onto Santa's lap a few times to share my secret wishes, hoping that perhaps God was listening, and my innocence might produce the impossible. Such are the dreams of children.

Our culture painted God as benevolent, much like Santa—jolly and just, always watching, always present, preparing gifts for me ... if only I was good.
Yet it was the "if" that made my heart tremble. I desperately yearned to be good, but I often felt like I fell short. The normal growing pains of childhood morphed into a harsh self-judgment and a nagging sense of inadequacy. I was "always" making a mess, and my best efforts seemed to result in greater chaos—or so I believed. Although I never heard a sermon likening God to an angry Santa, the messages I absorbed led me to that very conclusion. If I was good, God was pleased. If I was not—watch out ... I clung to a distorted belief that while God loved me, He was also perpetually disappointed in my immaturity.

In this context, every "bad" thing that happened felt like twisted divine retribution —a clear case of "reaping what I sowed." I want to be clear. These beliefs are lies. Lies believed will always make sense if left unchallenged. Could this truly encapsulate the heart of the God I wanted to serve? Where did grace and salvation fit into this picture? Was this the Jesus in scripture? I was just on the cusp of my teenage years, yearning for clarity, and unaware that these questions that felt so overwhelming, would actually lead me to the true Father.

Take Action

I will say this more than once. Honest questions asked in the presence of Father are one of the most powerful tools for transformation. Father. That's His whole name, and He wants you to know what He is like. Talk to Him. Expect to see something different.

Are you ready to shatter some mirrors? Which features do you think are a reflection of a flawed father figure or a poor understanding of His nature? Now for the exciting part: Invite Father to show you what He is really like. *Write it down.* We all have areas of distortion, or as the Apostle Paul says, "We see through a glass dimly." (See 1Cor. 13:12) Read the scripture below, and let the truth wash over you. You are found. Pursued. Loved.

> "Deep calls to deep at the sound of Your waterfalls; all Your breakers and Your waves have rolled over me. The LORD will command His lovingkindness in the daytime; and His song will be with me in the night, a prayer to the God of my life." –Psalm 42:7-8 NASB1995

The Prayer

Father God, adjust the mirrors so I can see You. Remove the distortion and jumbled beliefs with TRUTH. Untangle lies that hide in the immaturity and innocence of childhood. And restore the simple trust in You. Amen.

Are You a Father

Are You *like* a father?
Are You *like* my own?

My father loves us very much.
He works hard at church,
home, and job.
I barely see him.
He reads us stories every night.
Scary stories.
I like them.
Mom says he keeps us up
 too late at night.

Are *You* like a father?
Are *You* like my own?

My dad is perfect.
 I never see him fail.
  My father loves us very much.
   He works hard at
      church, at home,
         and at job.
      I barely know him.

We play sports!

He helps coach our game
   every Friday night.
 Sometimes I wonder—

*What is my dad really,
   really like...*

"Jesus said to him, 'Have I been so long with you, and yet you have not known Me, Philip? He who has seen Me has seen the Father ... '" —John 14:9 NKJV

"This is the true testimony: God has given us eternal life, and this life has its source in his Son. Whoever has the Son has eternal life; whoever does not have the Son does not possess eternal life." —1 John 5:11-12 TPT

My dad was a bit of a mystery to me growing up—kind and hard-working, yet still a mystery. He grew up without a father and had to work hard to shatter the lies and dysfunctional beliefs of his past. When he became a Christian, he dedicated a lot of time and prayer to this journey because he didn't want to pass on the brokenness he had experienced. It was a learning curve for both my parents, and I am so proud of them for committing to "walking the curve" and doing the hard work of being some of the first to become Christians in their family. I'm also grateful for their dedication; it was their passion for God that first inspired my own curiosity.

It only makes sense that God would begin to take on the same characteristics as my parents—kind, just, disciplinarian, and mysterious. I have this vivid memory of standing eagerly by a window for my dad to come home. It was late and dark, and I don't know why I was awake. Just a little kid in footie pajamas, waiting to run and hug Daddy when he walked in. That memory holds an intense feeling of missing him. I didn't see him much as a young kid; there isn't anything particularly dramatic about it—just that empty feeling of longing.

That feeling was normal. I didn't know what kind of relationship I wanted because I didn't understand what was possible. I was simply hungry. Jesus makes an interesting statement:

"'Blessed are those who hunger and thirst for righteousness,

For they shall be filled.'" Matthew 5:6 NKJV

God used my longing to know my earthly father to prepare me for my longing to know Him more.

Take Action

You have made us for yourself,
O Lord, and our heart is restless until it rests in you.– St. Augustine

It may not seem like a blessing to hunger, but it really is. Hunger signifies a longing, a desire for something greater. Have you ever noticed how, when we lose our appetite for the Kingdom of God, nothing satisfies and discontent becomes the norm? It's so easy to become complacent—allowing distractions to fill our days instead of seeking the richness of God's presence. Why not ask God to stir up that hunger again? Pray for a renewed desire to seek Him, to dive into His Word, and to embrace the blessings He offers.

Take some time to read Matthew 5, and let those truths wash over you. Take a moment to consider your own heart—what do you truly desire in your life? Is it peace, purpose, or deep friendship? Invite God into those desires, and ask Him to fill you with a deeper thirst for Him. Think about this for a moment: My longing to know my earthly father birthed the longing to know my Heavenly Father.

Everyone's story is different. I do not make light of the pain experienced when I say—there is hope. Let your hunger lead you to a relationship with Him you could not otherwise imagine. Embrace this journey; it's one worth taking.

The Prayer

Father,

Increase my hunger. Do not let me be satisfied with coping and surviving. Stir up a passion to pursue You. I choose to seek You with my whole heart. Fill me afresh and show me who You are. In the name of Jesus, Amen.

Something Exciting Happened

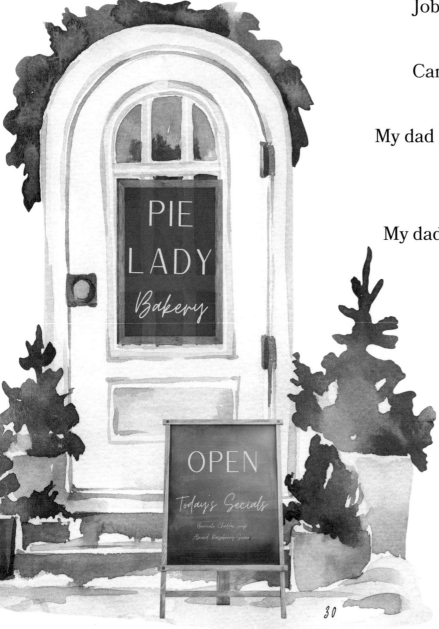

My dad lost his job.
He is very sad.
Jobs are hard to come by.

Can I tell you something?
Something exciting.
My dad is staying home today,

In the bakery.
My dad is going to help bake.

We make pies.
Peel apples.
Faster, Lisa.
Don't spill.
Careful now;
don't make a mess.
Slow down.
Pay attention.
BEEEEEEEEEP!!!!

Timer!
Hot pads!
Make space!
This is heavy.

Hot apple pies with beautiful golden crusts emerge.
But I don't even stop to look.
Roll 'em out!

Can I tell you something?

My dad lost his job for good today.
That means, tomorrow I get to see his smile, to hear
him laugh, to see his face.

But for today we clean for what seems like hours, and
we let the silence speak.

My dad understands silence.
He answers my unspoken questions.
Calms my whispered fears.
My dad, hears.
Although the world would say it is very sad to lose
your job this way ...
I hope it lasts for years and years and years.

The Journey

There was a season in my life when everything felt tumultuous. We moved away from my cozy cul-de-sac and close friends. The old neighborhood, filled with the joys of shared backyards, hide-and-seek, trips to the creek, daily playdates, and after-school games of Capture the Flag disappeared. We relocated to a small village with many neighbors but few children. Then my dad lost his job due to an injury. After several attempts at new ventures, it was decided that Mom's side hustle—the pie business—would become THE business.

At first, this seemed like a setback. Married couples aren't always the best business partners, and the food industry is tough. But it worked. As chaotic as that time was, having my dad around all the time was an answer to a prayer I didn't know I needed. We went from seeing him a couple of evenings a week to having him home all the time. I got to know him better.

As the shroud around my father lifted, I began to wonder again: What is God really like? It only made sense. Was God like the father I was getting to know—funny, quiet, reserved, strict, and kind? Our weekends were filled with markets, and baking occupied every day. This full life meant even as a young teen, I often felt tired and stressed. On the outside, I seemed to be thriving—well-adjusted and even-keeled. I loved the bakery, but I had no idea how to handle stress. Inside, the rug hiding my deepest feelings bulged painfully, demanding attention. I navigated crushes, friend drama, pimples, and periods. This emotional turmoil manifested as migraines and back pain, though I didn't connect the dots. The rug needed to go.

Do you ever feel a similar tension? What about those areas you carry that no one else sees and you may not even feel are worth mentioning? Unhealthy coping mechanisms can seem effective for a time, which is why we cling to them for so long. As we journey together, let's gently uncover those tough places and create space for Jesus to carry us through the rocky spaces.

Take Action

Meditate for a moment on your story. What was the routine of your growing-up years? Take a deep breath and allow memories to surface—those quiet moments of joy, the laughter shared, the challenges faced. How did your parents contribute to your view of God? Reflect on both the helpful and the not-so-helpful ways they influenced you.

Consider the warmth of their love, the lessons they imparted, and the ways they modeled faith. What moments filled your heart with hope? And on the other hand, were there times when their struggles cast shadows over your understanding of grace and love?

Ask God where He was in the midst of the ordinary. Can you see His hand in the small details of your daily life? How were those everyday experiences shaping you, and how are they still shaping you today?

Take time to journal your thoughts. Allow your pen to flow freely, capturing the beauty of your reflections and the tenderness of your heart. This is an opportunity to embrace your journey, recognizing that each moment has contributed to the person you are becoming. Invite God into your writing, asking Him to reveal deeper truths and insights as you explore your past.

Prayer

Father, here I am with a heart full of memories. Would You make the bitter sweet? I thank You for my story—the joys and challenges that have shaped me. Help me to see my growing-up years through Your eyes and to find Your presence woven through every moment of my life.

REVIVAL

The preacher says, "Passion like when you first met Jesus."
What if you never had any love at all?

The preacher says, "Return to love!"
I prayed the sinner's prayer when I was six.

What is passion?
What is first love?

I have never been in love.

Crushes, yes.
In love— no. Even I know, no
What is revival?
What draws the crowds and causes the people to shake?
What is the incessant conversation all around me about this invisible God
that so many want to,
so ardently
Stare in the face?

The Journey

Sozo (pronounced sode'-zo) From a primary sos (contraction for obsolete saos, "safe"); to save, i.e. deliver or protect (literally or figuratively):—heal, preserve, save (self), do well, be (make) whole. —Strong's Concordance

The Greek word for salvation is sozo.

Revival hit our area, bringing tent meetings, healings, and fresh enthusiasm for God. There weren't doors on these tents; they were open to the outside and drew larger crowds. I had never seen anything like it. Something amazing seemed to be happening. The more dynamic meetings often spoke about "first-love passion for the Lord." All the while, I wondered: What did it mean to "return to your first love"? How could I return to something I had never truly experienced and could barely comprehend? I prayed that prayer when I was so young. I knew I was saved, but it wasn't a life-changing experience for me. It was a prayer I recited to ensure I could go to heaven—There was no love in it.

I could imagine catching the eye of someone and leaving my corner of invisibility. Romantic love was the only template I had, but that seemed too shallow to be the topic of sermons. Not one to have many crushes, my most serious crush was a boy in my kindergarten class. He was amazing, with a great smile—though he drooled a lot. But that was okay. He played with me, and we were loners together. We would draw pictures, though I can't remember what else caught my eye. True love in kindergarten doesn't come with logic, and there was nothing in that experience to give context to the "first-love" others spoke about.

During these meetings, I was old enough to know that kindergartners don't fall in love; they have friends. Love is far more complicated and mysterious. It requires being seen. The love I longed for couldn't be attained without vulnerability, and the tug on my heart both excited and scared me. I yearned for someone to validate the space I took in the room. In the midst of  that longing, a new question formed: What if someone could see the invisible?

Take Action

This longing to be seen is beautifully demonstrated in the story of Hagar in Genesis 16. Hagar was in a place she didn't choose, facing hatred and rejection she didn't deserve. If anyone could have said she was "unseen," it was her. But God met her in that place. Pay close attention to her response in verse 13:

"Then she called the name of the LORD who spoke to her, 'You are God Who Sees'; for she said, 'Have I not even here [in the wilderness] remained alive after seeing Him [who sees me with understanding and compassion]?'" (Genesis 16:13 AMP)

God met Hagar at a spring in the desert. He saw this broken servant and answered the cry of her heart. In that place Hagar calls God "El Roi"—the God Who Sees. It is the only time the name is used. In her darkest place, she cried out to God and experienced sozo —salvation, healing, deliverance, and preservation. Hagar remained alive because God saw and spoke purpose into her place of greatest need.

When we cry out, God hears and sees. Take a minute to invite "El Roi" into your story today. He is the God who sees you.

Prayer

You are the God Who sees. You see me. I permit You to bring the hidden places of my heart into the light. I need You. I give up the identity of "invisible" and invite Your light. Thank You for seeing me and pursuing me. Amen.

Salvation

Light Changed
my World
Light wrecked
my view.
Light shook
my pride,
Love gave me
You.
You are God,
and I am a child.
You are Lover,
and You love wild.

The Journey

The moment was a tent meeting. The speaker preached, but honestly, I have no idea what he talked about. Having grown up in churches, I often found myself skeptical, with low expectations that anything "amazing" would happen to me. I can't recall the songs that filled the air, but at the end of the service, he said something that honestly felt cliché even to my young teen heart: "Someone is feeling a tug on their heart right now. If that is you, come up and give your heart to Jesus. Don't look around. Come back to your First Love."

As people began to go up front, I felt a pull inside me, like my heart was attached to a string that someone was gently tugging. A million questions swirled in my mind, mingling with fears and doubts. What if I looked foolish? What if I embarrassed myself? Yet, something lifted me out of my seat—A fire ignited in my heart that I couldn't ignore. With each step I took, I felt both excitement and apprehension. I remembered my earlier prayers and felt a twinge of embarrassment because I knew my parents were watching. What would they think of me coming forward again? Yet, despite my fears, I couldn't deny the pull I felt. I hoped that maybe the answer to all my questions lay in this tiny yes.

A tiny yes. That's all it takes. An act of agreement that speaks louder than the doubts. It's a moment that moves heaven and earth. While I believe I was "saved" before that day, there was something uniquely transformative in that second confession. This was my decision—a stake in the ground. I believed the restless longings of my heart could be satisfied. It was an amazing moment.

Salvation is a precious gift. Whether it's for the first time or you are many years into the journey, let's take a moment to affirm our connection today and embrace the love that calls us back to Him.

Take Action

Have you given your heart to Jesus? Christians often use the term "get saved," but what does that really mean? I love the completeness that we saw shown in the Greek word *sozo*. That wholeness is what Jesus purchased when He took our punishment and offered us the opportunity to live a life that is safe, whole, healed, saved, and delivered. This process always begins with the gentle drawing of the Holy Spirit.

Have you felt that pull of love? Today is your day. Whether it's for the first time or a rededication, today is the day to be made whole.

Prayer

Papa, I believe that Jesus died for my sins. I surrender my life to You and receive Your forgiveness. I need You. Thank You for making me Your child. Thank You for the fullness of sozo filling my heart today. Do beyond what I can think or ask. For Your glory, amen.

"No one can come to Me unless the Father who sent Me draws him [giving him the desire to come to Me] ..." John 6:44a AMP

"This is my beloved, this is my friend ..."
Song of Songs 5:16b NIV

LIGHT

I was in the corner.

I was in the back row.
I was unseen,
invisible.

I was strong.
I was constant,
calm.
I was alone.

I was un-
You were love.
I was un-
You were love.

Then *You* saw
me.
Then I saw
You.
Then You
touched me.
Then I *saw*
You.

I was in the
back corner,
Hiding in the
back row,
Unseen,
invisible.

Then You saw me.

Light came again. The room, jam-packed with people, had a handful of seats left. Instead of sitting with my mom while my dad was with the leadership team, all the teens and the overflow of guests stood in the back of the room. Little cliques of friends quickly formed. I could have joined any of them, but my self-imposed segregation habit left me standing alone. Genuinely interested in what was happening in the service, I also purposefully distanced myself from the distracted chatter. I was not wanting to spend the evening in whispered conversation or angling for someone's attention.

The whole night was a service with prayer, song, and scripture reading. The girl leading worship sang a song called, "Your Love Is Extravagant." She swayed to the music, closed her eyes, and as I watched her, I too realized—She is really singing to Jesus. She really means this. My heart swelled. This was what I wanted. This was the longing for which I had no words. I wanted to know the God Who loved me passionately and completely without strings attached.

Then suddenly, the music paused, and someone read Song of Solomon 2. When it ended with, "This is my beloved, this is my friend," the realness of Jesus sank into my heart. He looked like something. He was not this vague thing to loosely hold onto—He had substance. He wanted to be my friend. He wanted me to know I was loved. He loved me. So simple. So innocent. So pure. But believing this changed everything.

There was no moonlight or magical sparkle; there was just the light that shone on a young girl still wrestling with the desire to be invisible. The Prince came. Jesus wanted to be my friend. He saw me. He saw everything, and He invited me into something entirely new. This was a new idea—that my longings for love could be met by God. Not in friends, a boyfriend or by stuffing them into some future corner of my heart. Love—a wild, consuming love—had entered the room and would give confidence where there had been shame and speak affirmation where lies had lived. I came unlocked. And when I came unlocked, years of words poured out of my mouth. I was bubbling with words when we got to the car.

The Journey

For ten minutes of the twenty-minute ride home, I poured out more words than my parents had ever heard me say at one time. I was beyond excited about the revelation. God was not an angry Santa—He loved me! I wanted everyone to know this amazing love. The girl who had always lived to be hidden talked and talked. For a moment, there was healing in the release. I felt brave and visible. But the path never runs in a straight line. My sweet father did what so many fathers do so innocently—he teased me. And the weight of those words nearly crushed my tender heart.

I got home and rushed to my room, refusing to let anyone see the tears that threatened as I dug my bare toes into the little rug. *Hide. Don't cry.*

At that moment, I made a decision. I replayed all that I had experienced and realized I could not let go of the love I knew was real. The tangle was that I also believed it would be better to be silent. The lie I embraced was that talking only meant I would be misunderstood. That's how the enemy works. He comes in right beside our breakthrough to discourage us and cause us to question. But when we know that's what the enemy does, we can fight smarter and better wield the power of belief.

Take Action

"This is my beloved, this is my friend." (Song of Solomon 5:16 NIV)

Read Song of Solomon 5:10-16. It is amazing to think that Jesus looks like something. I am a visual person, so I often see pictures as I read or hear words. With God, though, I had taken the jumble of things I had heard and remembered about Him and made a picture of this slightly angry Santa-God who put on a jolly front, but, in reality, was just frustrated with the sinfulness of His kids. That night at the tiny church building, as that passage was read, the truth burned in my heart: "This is my beloved, this is *my* friend." (emphasis mine) Jesus wants to be OUR Friend. He wants to be the *substance* of all we are hoping for and the *evidence* of everything unseen. Take a moment right now to invite Him into your space.

Prayer

Father, I welcome You here. Shift what needs shifting. Break what needs breaking. Heal what needs healing. And give me boldness to share Your love. Most of all, be my Friend.

PARADIGM

SHIFT

I have been so good to
please You.
I have feared the coal an
angry Santa-God would
leave.
I have been so good to
please You.
You have been so pleased
to be good to me.
You took off the heavy
overcoat I had put on You.
You showed me Your
hands, Your face, Your
eyes.
And all of love pierced
through me. Love saw
everything I tried to hide.
In these arms, this child is
falling,
Falling into arms open
Wide.

The Journey

Change takes time. Being childlike means being willing to be in process. Where hiding and stuffing had been the norm for me, with each new revelation, I relaxed into a deeper trust. I realized I could believe Jesus above all the other feelings, and that was powerful. I remember sitting in the middle of my bedroom, closing my eyes, and picturing those burning eyes of love again. Words still stung. I still felt incredibly awkward. I felt afraid. But like smooth, round stones, I held each revelation:

He loves me.

I believe it.

He sees me.

How could I deny those eyes?

He is not an angry Santa.

I almost laughed remembering that one. ... *No, not an angry Santa.*

Life didn't change overnight, but those memorial stones were truths that defeated giants in my life. I could linger in that space—perfectly in process. Sometimes we put so much pressure on ourselves to get everything right that we forget that being childlike means embracing the messy with joy.

A story about Mary (not the mother of Jesus) in the Bible has captured my heart. Mary, friend of Jesus, bucked social norms and chose to sit at His feet (See Luke 10:38-42). She had a choice, and she chose to stay present with Jesus, no matter the cost. Similarly, Mary made the choice again when she poured costly oil on the feet of Jesus. Her seemingly wasteful act of honor still teaches us today.

When we bring our most precious things and choose to open our hearts to Jesus, giving Him everything in worship—It's worth it. As we look back on our journeys, remember that every little step, every choice we make, and every moment spent in rest and trust brings us closer to the love and freedom Jesus has for us. Just like Mary, we can choose to be present with Him, no matter what's going on around us—It's all part of the journey.

So, take a moment to let His love wash over you. Know that your offerings, no matter how big or small, matter. You are stepping into something beautiful. This is the heart of worship, and it's worth every bit of vulnerability.

> "'Mary has discovered the one thing most important by choosing to sit at my feet. She is undistracted, and I won't take this privilege from her.'" —Luke 10:42 (TPT)

Take Action

Vows are powerful, and change takes time. I made vows to hide that took years to untangle. Mary could have vowed to never be so bold again and missed the opportunity to pour the oil on Jesus' feet (See Luke 10 and Mathew 26:6-13).

Take a moment to write down a vow you've made that isn't serving your heart or allowing you to rest and trust. Invite God into that space and listen for His voice; you might hear comforting words or simply the gentle rhythm of your heartbeat. Let it beat—It's a sign of life returning.

Imagine Him gently removing the heavy overcoat of false expectations, revealing His loving gaze and open arms. Allow yourself to feel the warmth of His love piercing through the walls you've built.

Ask, "What do You want me to know about You?" Remember, you are cherished —not for what you do, but simply because you are His.

Prayer

Father, I ask that You open our eyes and hearts to know where we have made vows—knowingly or unknowingly—that contradict Your will. Holy Spirit, I invite You to lead and guide me into all truth, and may I feel Your love and grace as I uncover these truths. For Your name's sake. Amen.

"This I recall to my mind, Therefore I have hope. The Lord's lovingkindnesses indeed never cease, For His compassions never fail. They are new every morning; Great is Your faithfulness. 'The Lord is my portion,' says my soul, 'Therefore I have hope in Him.'"
Lamentations 3:21-24 NASB1995

May I Have This Dance

I am awake. What is this feeling?

What is this love?
The moon is shining brightly–too brightly.

I am awake.
What is this changing?
This growing hunger deep inside.

I remember standing in that corner and seeing Jesus' eyes.

I am there again. I am in the passion again.
In the sight of handsome, holy God pursuing awkward, chubby me.

And in the moon is light, and I move to the song that heaven plays.

And I dance alone with my new Friend.

48

"May I have this dance?

May I stay with you tonight?

I want to stay here, forever.

There have been feelings,

that you've tried to fight,

But all I want to do

is to dance tonight."

The Journey

When I closed my eyes, I saw the eyes that Scripture speaks of—fiery and piercing, looking right at me. They were ablaze yet kind, searching deeply into my soul—not through me or past me. His gaze stopped at me. The kindness in His eyes was a far cry from the grumpy Santa I had made God out to be. There was passion in His eyes. Passion and compassion—for me. It changed me.

I would often wake up in the middle of the night and simply sit in the wonder that I was loved. I would read my Bible, journal, and pray. There was no compulsion; I just wanted to spend that time.

Even in my hiding, Father God was faithful. He wasn't distracted by my broken ways. He was intent on teaching me that He was a safe place to be seen. He would peel back the rug one day, but in that moment, He was pleased to pursue me, to sit with me in my childish brokenness, until time proved Trust, and healing would come.

There is more. Whatever you have experienced—There is more. Jesus didn't die on the cross for boring religion. He came to show us the Father. He came for friends. (See John 15:15) I challenge you: Don't be satisfied—Hunger and thirst for more.

Take Action

I love Jesus. One of the most transformational things that occurred that night was that my faith became real, tangible—personal experience and not just good ideas. This is not something we can conjure up or pray until a feeling comes. No, this is a God-moment where what has been routine or dry comes alive. Invite Jesus into your space. Get hungry—for real. The next time you wake up and feel that gnawing sensation that is the need for nourishment: PAUSE. Reflect. No matter how much apathy, indifference, boredom, or confusion you may feel toward spending time with God or reading the Bible, remember this: Your soul is hungry. Desperately hungry, and it will only be satisfied by Him

Prayer

Father, I am hungry for You. Would You sit with me tonight and teach my heart to trust again? Remove any fear and every word spoken over my life that seeks to steal my joy. Help me to see what Love says about me—I am enough, I matter, and I am valued. Amen.

FEAR

I am different.
I am changed.
I wring my hands and look
around.
I am pregnant with a passion.
Will the world mock me now?
I am afraid.
I've been afraid for a long
time.
How long does it take to
change one's name?

It is painful to be different.
I will be quiet instead.
That has worked well all
these years.
I will be quiet, secret Lisa.
Undisturbed and
Without fear.
But I have this nagging little
longing
That forms a question on my
lips,
What if in all this hiding—
passion becomes fear?

"If I say, 'I will not
mention him,
or speak any more
in his name,'
there is in my heart
as it were a burning
fire
shut up in my
bones,
and I am weary
with holding it in,
and I cannot."
Jeremiah 20:9 ESV

The Journey

I had a choice. Transition. I was moving from questions and wondering to knowing and experiencing. The challenge was, would I allow the fear of being seen, misunderstood, or even momentarily embarrassed to silence me? I remember reading through parables and coming to the sections where Jesus talks about us being the salt of the earth and how no one takes a light and puts it under a bushel.

In Matthew 5:13-14 (ESV), it says: "'You are the salt of the earth, but if salt has lost its taste, how shall its saltiness be restored? It is no longer good for anything except to be thrown out and trampled under people's feet. You are the light of the world. A city set on a hill cannot be hidden.'"

The conclusion Jesus makes for tasteless salt and hidden lights is that they are good for nothing—and that hit me hard. I was scared of being misunderstood, so I largely kept silent. I didn't talk about God much with my friends, but I wondered if I continued to hide, would what I experienced become good for nothing—tasteless? Would I trade the revelation of being seen and known by God for the supposed comfort of being understood by others? Would I deny Christ? These are weighty questions for a young teen, but I was faced with a choice, so very timidly, I said, "I choose You, Jesus. Teach me how to not be so afraid." This was my surrender. It was a surrender I would make over and over again over the years, but the most powerful thing about this journey is the momentum that obedience brings.

Take Action

Take a moment and tell Jesus what your heart needs. What fears would drive your light under a bushel and the taste from who God made you to be? The world needs who you were created to be. If the enemy cannot get you to walk away from God, he will try to get you to walk alone. Connecting with others doesn't have to be complicated. This may look like deciding to call a friend to pray with, hosting a Bible story, or telling your testimony casually to a relative or friend at the next holiday gathering. Let's take a step toward transparency and become fearless.

Prayer

Dear Jesus,
You say You see me. I need to be seen by You. You say You know me. I need to be known by You. Take the fear that is grasping for control. I surrender.
Amen.

FEAR-less

The fears that kept me locked inside were the voices that said,

Every dream you dream is wrong.
Difficulty means failure.
Grow up and change your song.

But a bird is born to fly, and mine were eagle wings,
 and I could not change my song.

Fear kept me ashamed inside, and the voices that said,

Every dream you
could dream better.

Your vision could be better.
Rise up and sing this song.

But a bird that is born to fly must fly
high, and I cannot change the song.

Something deep inside is burning.
Something deep inside is *singing*.
Something deep inside is saying,

It is not too late.

Quenched and quelled. Forgotten and
forsaken.
Hope deferred and waiting here.
Quenched and quelled. Forgotten and
forsaken.
Hope deferred but not forsaken.
A burning flame
A flash of light
A burning pain, a flash of light.

You are coming free.

The Journey

You are coming free.

Over the years, deliverance has often been misused and abused. Its true meaning—the simple act of being set free from what holds us captive—has been muddied. When Mary Magdalene stood free of demons for the first time, as described in Luke 8, I wonder what she felt.

To be in her right mind again, to feel and think without the torment of seven demons breathing, scheming, and clawing inside her. What was that first clear breath like? No wonder she followed Jesus. While I do not know Mary's pain nor do I have her dramatic story, I do know freedom and what it is like to breathe without the weight of lies—shame and unworthiness—pressing in.

I wonder what Lazarus thought as he stumbled through the cave, obeying the command of his friend. Wrapped in grave clothes, who loosed his bands? Who helped him bathe? He stood both resurrected and in such need. Freedom is both a glorious moment and a process. The enemy would like us to believe when the wonder wears off that mediocracy and rote obedience is all there is left. And that is not true. There are seasons for everything, including deliverance.

We don't need to have Lazarus' story to tremble as the King of the universe says, "Come out!" and breathe the clean, cool air that fills our lungs when heaviness melts away. Over the years, I've known what it's like to be surrounded by an army of friends who pray and speak healing and freedom when I could not. Freedom is not found alone; it is known in the kind words of friends who speak the truth of who we are in Christ. To experience and KNOW this changes everything.

"Stop imitating the ideals and opinions of the culture around you, but be inwardly transformed by the Holy Spirit through a total reformation of how you think. This will empower you to discern God's will as you live a beautiful life, satisfying and perfect in his eyes." Romans 12:2 TPT

Take Action

Lies we believe act like chains that lock us on our journey. But when the truth breaks the power of those lies, deliverance happens. Deliverance means release from captivity, slavery, oppression, or any restraint (see Webster's 1828 Dictionary). Lies are like cages; they trap us in a reality that does not exist in Heaven. Jesus came to 'proclaim the favorable year of the Lord' and 'to set the captives free' (Isaiah 61:1, Luke 4:18). Deliverance sets us free.

Our journey is moving from one way of thinking to another. Ask God to silence the voice of Fear and to remove the lies that Fear has woven into your reality. Then, invite Him to show you the truth.

"For He rescued us from the domain of darkness, and transferred us to the kingdom of His beloved Son." (Colossians 1:13 NASB1995)

Bookmark these steps to freedom. As you experience the joy that release brings, you'll want to return to this place often.

Step 1: Acknowledge and Let Go
Take a moment to recognize any beliefs that weigh you down and bring them to God in prayer. Remember 1 John 1:9—He's always ready to forgive!

Step 2: Get Clean and Bless
Plead the blood of Jesus over your past and release any burdens you've been carrying. Forgive whomever you need to forgive—especially yourself. Remember, words are powerful. Shift happens as you speak truth over yourself, your situations, and your relationships.

Step 3: Invite the Holy Spirit
Ask the Holy Spirit to fill your heart and guide you in truth. Trust that He is working in you, helping you grow the beautiful fruit of the Spirit in your life (John 16:13)

Prayer

I decree that who the Son sets free is free indeed and ALL that the enemy has attempted to steal is being returned because of the blood and resurrection of Jesus Christ. Father, I thank you for making this precious one know and believe the love you have for them and the inheritance they have in You. I ask that you provide godly counsel and a friend to walk alongside them so that they can function in your family as they pursue healing. Amen.

Friends and mentors are essential. Seek out good counsel and commit to the process (not necessarily an instant work but a faithful process) of honesty and healing. There is power when we pray with someone else for freedom. One can chase a thousand, two can chase ten thousand (See Deuteronomy 32:30). The difference is exponential. Don't go alone. Trust that God will use even flawed people—like you and me—to further your healing. If you are in a situation of abuse or battling the issues of depression and suicide, do not hesitate to get professional help.

First Love

Part 1

You came into my room today,

The one inside my head.

You pointed to the rug today,

The one inside my room.

You saw that I was very scared.

You did not look ashamed.

You sat me by your feet today,
    by the rug, inside my room.

    You peeled back the rug today,
      the one inside my head.

    You saw that I was very scared.
      and then You cried one giant tear

and better than invisible,
You let me cry all my tears,
And made all the hurt go away.

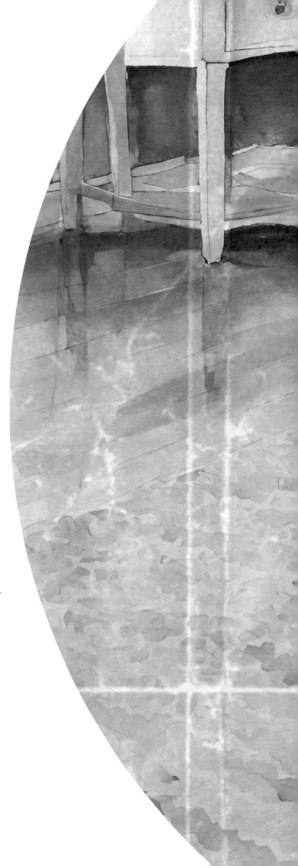

The Journey

This topic takes a bit of unpacking, so I am going to do something a little different and break "The Journey" into two parts. Feel free to read at the pace that works for you. May this be a space to go deeper with God.

There comes a day when we must face the rug in our room. I had lived with the "sweep it under the rug" coping habit for so long that I had forgotten how unhealthy it was. Have you ever gotten so comfortable with a habit that it ceases to feel strange? I once heard a story about a woman who had her bathroom remodeled. Everything was wonderful—except when the contractor left, she discovered that to make the hot water work, the back flood lights needed to be turned on. Instead of calling the contractor back, she just lived with this oddity. One day, her sister visited from out of town and needed to take a shower. There's nothing like having fresh eyes to reveal the truth about a situation. After experiencing the inconvenience of having to shout for someone to "turn on the floodlights" to get hot water, this faithful sister leaned in and said, "I hope you know—that's not normal."

There are things we tolerate in our lives that should not be considered "normal," especially when they do not reflect the kingdom of Heaven. It reminds me of the powerful moments when we allow God's light to shine into our hidden places, revealing truths we often ignore. How ridiculous would it be for the visiting sister to leave thinking, "I'm never remodeling my bathroom—I don't want to turn my floodlights on for hot water"? We would laugh at the absurdity. And yet, we make vows to never go to church again, never pursue relationships, never have children—never _____ (you fill in the blank)—all because someone else's tolerance for something that was never meant to be has taken its toll on *our* lives. It shouldn't be that way.

Just as Jesus calls us to step into the light, we are invited to let go of the burdens of fear and shame. We can embrace the truth of being seen and known by God. It's time to confront the "rug."

Take Action

1. Ask God to reveal to you His thoughts. What is God's "normal"?

2. Where has dysfunction become normal for you? Is it an abusive relationship? Poor food choices? Is the tone you speak to others unhealthy? Commit to a new normal today. Write it down.

3. Read Philippians 4.
After you've soaked in the words, take a moment to meditate on verses 6-7: How can prayer and gratitude reshape your thoughts? Grab your journal and reflect on what you're thankful for. What worries do you need to hand over to God today?

"Be cheerful with joyous celebration in every season of life. Let your joy overflow! ... Don't be pulled in different directions or worried about a thing. Be saturated in prayer throughout each day, offering your faith-filled requests before God with overflowing gratitude. Tell him every detail of your life, and then God's wonderful peace that transcends human understanding, will guard your heart and mind through Jesus Christ. Keep your thoughts continually fixed on all that is authentic and real, honorable and admirable, beautiful and respectful, pure and holy, merciful and kind. And fasten your thoughts on every glorious work of God, praising him always. Put into practice the example of all that you have heard from me or seen in my life and the God of peace will be with you in all things." Philippians 4:4, 6-9 TPT

The Prayer

Father,
Open my eyes to the areas where I've tolerated dysfunction in my life. Help me pull back the rug of hidden emotions and guide me through the feelings I've avoided. I choose to trust You. Amen.

First Love

Part 2

"There is an appointed time
for everything.
And there is a time for
every event
under heaven."
—Ecclesiastes 3:1

NASB1995

"Jesus wept."
John 11:35

NASB1995

As I trusted God with all that was inside of me, He brought the healing. Not justification. Not retribution—healing. I knew the pain of a bulging rug . And into that space, Jesus sat. Instead of scolding me,
He simply said, *"Come to Me."*

There was a season when I poured over the story of Mary and Martha in the Bible (See Luke 10). I can relate to both women. I worked in a bakery, and my mom catered occasionally on the side. To sit and not help when guests were around was unimaginable—I would be ticked, too. But to be numbered among the very few who had the honor of sitting at Jesus' feet? That was a longing I knew well. How did these women maneuver through all the feelings they experienced? How did they forgive each other—and themselves?

Forgiveness is a powerful act, and it's something we hear about often. Sometimes it can seem like we're just being told to "ignore" or "excuse" the wrongs done to us. Hurts happen. Some people ask for forgiveness but only seem to be looking for a free pass on their actions. That can be tough. When wrongs occur, it often feels like the only choices are to get bitter or to hide those feelings under the rug again.

Many of us become so used to hiding our true selves that we might start believing our pain doesn't matter. It's easy to adopt a belief system that seems to work on the surface: If I feel hurt, that's my problem—Just forgive and move on. But to hold onto that belief, we often have to accept another lie: that God doesn't care about our hearts or experiences. The truth is, God isn't afraid of our feelings. He gave us emotions for a reason.

That is what made that moment on the tiny rug in my room so powerful. Somewhere along the way—whether from well-meaning teaching or misunderstanding—I learned that emotions should be contained and not trusted

Negative emotions became sin. Anger or frustration meant a lack of patience and peace. Sadness suggested I was not choosing joy. *Not True.* While emotions can be terrible taskmasters, they're also God-given gauges that help us understand the season we're in and what our hearts need.

These days, I tend a large garden. It would be unwise for me to ignore the signs of an impending storm or to think I can control the weather with sheer willpower. Similarly, it's foolish to ignore what's affecting our hearts. Neither Mary nor Martha let fear or shame keep them from bringing their whole hearts to Jesus again and again. (See John 11:17-35 and Matthew 26:5-13)

It is a beautiful picture to think that forgiveness can look like Martha's bold honesty and Mary's costly oil poured at Jesus' feet—no hesitancy, no hiding.

Take Action

This step takes bravery. Have you been afraid of the emotions inside? Have you found it easier to pretend? Remember, God wants you to feel again. Before you can truly know the joy of freedom, you may need to face some pain. Sometimes that means embracing the truth about an unhealthy relationship and calling it what it is—toxic. Or it might involve confessing that a behavior you once excused is actually hurting you and those you love.

God is a safe place to bring your whole self home. Spend some time reading about Mary and Martha mentioned in the scriptures above.
Get honest. Honesty is key. Speak the truth to yourself and to God. Confess. You can only reap the rewards of your trials if you give yourself permission to go through the hard times. God wants all of your heart. All of it. It all matters.

Take a moment to ask God to help you feel again. It's time. Experience another layer of deliverance—you are coming free. In this space, allow yourself to forgive.

Prayer

In the name of Jesus, I break the fear and shame that would cling to this precious child of Yours, and I plead the blood of Jesus over their mind and memories. Heal the areas of deepest pain, and give them courage and strength to go through the trials with You. And in doing so, may they experience abundant joy.

Who Is Father

What or who is Father?

To whom do you refer?

I just don't know *my* father.

Not very well.

Not very much.

He is loving.

His discipline we fear.

But who is Father—Father God?

The man you died to show?

Jesus, special Friend, for I can now call You this,

Who is Father?

Psalm 131 AMP

Childlike Trust in the Lord

"LORD, my heart is not proud, nor my
eyes haughty;
Nor do I involve myself in great matters,
Or in things too difficult for me.
Surely I have calmed and quieted my
soul;
Like a weaned child [resting] with his
mother,
My soul is like a weaned child within me
[composed and freed from discontent].
O Israel, hope in the LORD
From this time forth and forever."

The Journey

Take a deep breath. Does the air feel different here? Newly free and full of childlike wonder, I asked the question Jesus loves to hear: Who is Father? My dad wasn't perfect and didn't pretend to be, but he was all I knew. I wanted to know more about the God Who was beyond what I could see. *Show me the Father.*

The question flowed out of this new place of freedom and rest. I felt the pull to "be right" and "do right," and I still felt the fear of being misunderstood, but I was changing. The most surprising and beautiful thing was that with change came a fullness of joy. I talked to my friends about what God was doing in my life. I talked! Sometimes we had meaningful conversations, and sometimes it was awkward. But instead of picturing a rug, I envisioned a lamp on a hill. When I was tempted to hide (and I often still was), I reminded myself that I was meant to be a light, and my choices could extinguish or dim the gift inside.

"... if you have seen me, you have seen the Father ..." (John 14:9b NASB)

This is where my mind went tilt. The same passionate, deep-knowing love I felt when encountering Jesus was the love the Father had for me. The Father loved me. The Father LOVES me. He was not in a hurry or unknowable. With that revelation, I realized I did not have a Father sitting, waiting to judge me, but a Father sitting in the room, wanting to process all the feelings.
So for hours, I sat in my room, listening to music, reading my Bible, or journaling. I would write about the good and the bad, and sometimes I would just sit, absorbing the light. And that felt so much better than a lumpy rug.

Take Action

Soak in the Father's affirmation. You are beautiful. Your countenance has changed; there's a lightness in your eyes that wasn't there before, and your smile radiates vibrancy. You are gorgeous. I may not see your face, but I know—because I've experienced it myself. It's tangible.

Take a moment to reflect on your journey. Look through photos of yourself and notice how you've transformed. Each image captures not just your outward appearance, but the growth and resilience you've cultivated along the way. Or simply stand in front of the mirror and say thank you—to God, for His unfailing love, and to your own heart for being brave enough to embrace this journey.

You are becoming the truest version of yourself, shedding old layers and revealing the beauty that has always been within you. Celebrate this moment. You are beautiful.

Prayer

Let me pray over you today.

*Father, I ask that You hold Your precious one today. May they
see the beauty You are weaving as You redeem their story.
Thank You for being faithful. Amen.*

"Consider it all joy, my brethren, when you encounter various trials, knowing that the testing of your faith produces endurance. And let endurance have its perfect result, so that you may be perfect and complete, lacking in nothing." — James 1:2-4 NASB1995

"Trust in him at all times, you people; pour out your hearts to him, for God is our refuge." — Psalm 62:8 (NIV)

Just Beginning

Dear Father, Papa God,
I can trust You with my
deepest fears.
I can trust You with the pain.
I can trust You with the
loneliness.
I can trust You with the shame.
I can trust You.
I didn't realize how much I
was afraid.

As I entered my teen years, I juggled school and jobs, discovering a whole new world opening up before me. The older I grew, the more I began to open up. In high school, people remarked on my maturity and commented on "what a lovely young lady I was becoming." Yet inwardly, I chafed at the idea. I hadn't figured out how maturity and childlike wonder could coexist. There was still a part of me that didn't want to become a "battle-hardened" adult.

But another shift was happening. The tangled threads of my life were beginning to form a tapestry. A tapestry is formed from seemingly discordant threads. As God removed the lies and redeemed my memories, that tapestry—all of it— became beautiful.

One day, while driving, a question popped into my head: *Would you give your money away?* I assumed it was God asking, and my heart immediately responded, "Yes! Where!?" Money was something I loved to give. But then came the next question: *Would you give away one million dollars?* Again, I replied, "Yes, but You'd have to give me a million dollars first." I was being cheeky, but that's when God whispered, *That's right. It's impossible to give what you don't have. If you don't see yourself as I see you and believe what I say about you, you won't be able to truly see or believe the best in others. If you cannot be patient with yourself, you won't be patient with others. If you cannot forgive yourself, you won't be able to forgive others. Lisa, if you don't take the plank out of your own eye, you cannot speak into the lives of others. You cannot give what you do not have.*

Only God can speak such words without a hint of condemnation or guilt. Suddenly healing became about more than just me. It became about the friends I wanted to love well, the future children I would raise, and the daughter I wanted to be. *I can't give what I don't have.* With that phrase in my heart, the journey turned outward. I was on this path for more than just myself.

Take Action

The threads of our history can sometimes seem like a hopeless tangle. But when the Master Weaver comes, hope ignites as the fabric takes shape, revealing that God has been at work all along. Those broken threads have a purpose; what felt like reckless cutting was truly the careful crafting of His hand.

If you can, take a moment to look up weaving—it's a beautiful art form filled with life lessons. Breathe. Remember, a tapestry is designed to tell a story. Ask God to highlight someone you can share your journey with. Your light is needed.

Prayer

Father, I choose to trust You. I give You the places in my heart I have been holding back. Make something beautiful out of every pain. I give my heart permission to feel and not ignore. Keep me vulnerable to Your shaping. I want to be fully Yours. I trust You. Amen.

TALENT-LESS

See Mathew 25:14-30 ESV

*For the kingdom of heaven will be like a man going on a journey
who called his servants and entrusted to them his property...and talents of silver...*

I cannot sing a melody that others want to hear
but songs fill my heart.

I sing in the basement, shower ... at work.
Too loudly at work.

I speak but the words are jumbled.
Eyebrows raise.
I am not sure they understand.
I do not read well.
Do not ask me to read out loud.

I have no burning drive to do
or be something very great.
I have no extraordinary skill.

I am a hard worker
I work three jobs—
Bakery, babysitting,
farm market.
I save my money.
I wear my sister's clothes.
In my hand I hold nothing
but this passion for children
and for You.
What can I do?
I am 16. I am talentless.

But maybe, I have one?
Maybe ...
*I will spend it all on passion.
One talent.
I will take one risk.
Here is one talent,
Jesus I am spending it all on You.*

"So above all, constantly seek God's kingdom and his righteousness, then all these less important things will be given to you abundantly." Matthew 6:33 TPT

I heard a teaching about talents that impacted my 14-year-old life forever. I had this little cassette tape (Who remembers those?!) that I listened to over and over. The speaker, also a young person, made the case that the teen years offer a unique opportunity to invest our time and energy into developing skills for our future. He encouraged teens to channel their restless energy and creativity into a practical skill or hobby they loved. Even if they never became a star football player or pursued music or art professionally, the skills developed through perseverance and practice are invaluable gifts.

As we reflect on the different seasons of life, the teen years provide a unique opportunity that doesn't repeat itself. Ages one through twelve are spent learning the basics of life—how to eat, use the toilet, read, and so on. From twelve to eighteen, we grow in independence while still having the safety net of home. Then comes the stage from eighteen to thirty, which typically involves college, careers, and perhaps even marriage and family. After thirty, we face the pressures of careers and increasing responsibilities.

While skill-building and pursuing passions later in life is certainly possible, it becomes more complex. Most 12 to 18-year-olds are in a special period where they can cultivate skills and explore interests without the burden of providing for themselves or their families. However, what the speaker didn't address was what to do if someone feels their life was boring. I didn't have a passion. I worked three jobs, I wrote, and I read. I became more active during my teens, but I wasn't into sports. Having spent so many years hiding, I didn't even know what I liked.

I found myself in that space once again, feeling inadequacy wrap its arms around me and whispering feelings of unworthiness. Scanning the future, the idea of being a monk—someone who lived alone in the woods with God—sounded ideal.

Old habits coddled insecurity, yet Love was present to combat the lies this time. That is the beauty of doing life with God: The lies don't stick as easily. One of my hobbies was art. Armed with the intention to practice drawing and watercolor for the sake of discipline, I began to explore my creative side. While drawing one day, a thought popped into my head: "How would an artist feel if someone gushed over them but showed no appreciation or interest in the art?" Can you imagine someone walking through an art gallery, ignoring the artwork but fawning over the artist? Instantly, I realized God was teaching me a lesson. Even in my unskilled state, I would feel put off and perceive that kind of attention as insincere.

God doesn't make bad art. My talents or gifts may not be evident to me yet, but I would not insult God by calling myself His "oops painting." Since I trusted the Master Artist of my life, the correct response on my part would be to sit with Him and ask, "Tell me about this painting."

In that moment, an idea formed: *What if I threw myself into knowing the Artist? Maybe if I studied His work and get to know His thoughts that could be something.* And what if, by pursuing Him, my life would fall into place? The truth was right in front of me, but I still wasn't sure until one night while babysitting. Looking for something decent on TV. I flipped through the channels until I landed on a preacher speaking from Matthew 6:33: "'Seek first the kingdom of God, and all these things will be added to you.'"

It clicked. It wasn't just a good idea—It was a promise. I may not know what the future holds, but I could know Him. This was my one talent.

Take Action

Read the Parable of the Talents in Matthew 25:14-30.

I appreciate the play on words here. In the parable, talents were the currency of the day, referring to coins. In modern times, our talents—skills and abilities—act very much like currency. What skills has God given you? He wants to use your gifts to reveal who He is and what He has created you for (see Ephesians 1). So, give your talents back to God. No matter your age, let the pursuit of Christ be the talent you invest in, the skill you develop, and the passion you pursue.

And if you don't yet see the gifts God has given you, set your heart to seek the Lord. The Great Artist is eager to reveal the beauty He created in you. God is the Creator of creators, and we bear His image.

Prayer

Holy Spirit, You see me and know me. Show me what You see when You look at me. Forgive me for devaluing Your creation—both myself and others. I want to testify to what You have done and who You have made me to be. I set my heart to seek You first. What are Your thoughts about me and those around me? Thank You. Amen.

(Where Do People Go?)

Where do people go when they leave this holy building?
We sing the song.
We celebrate.
And then somehow, somewhere ... They slip away.

I thought I knew you.

And then somehow, somewhere ... They slip away.
Where do people go when they journey far from here?
Where do people go?
My heart aches.
I do not understand.
And then again, I do.
I miss them.
I miss you.

Dear God.

Where do we go when we leave this building?
What adventure do You have for me?
Your eyes are still sparkling.
Your eyes are still calling.
Your eyes are still wet.
You feel the pain, too.
You know exactly where everyone is.

The Journey

There is no pain like watching someone you care about walk away from the love of God. The greatest pain of my teen years was watching friends choose different paths. I had been given a life-shifting experience with God. It was confusing and even shocking at times as the differences in our lives grew greater and greater. I struggled with guilt. I wrestled with the questions like: Was God just? Was I special? Maybe if I did something different, friendships wouldn't fade. The thread of a false sense of responsibility needed pulling. I could save no one. My questions were born out of a desire to figure out and "make right." But I was not supposed to do that. I would never be the central actor in anyone's story. That responsibility sat solidly on Jesus' shoulders.

In The Horse and His Boy, one of C.S. Lewis's Narnia stories, Shasta asks why his friend Aravis experienced pain. Aslan, who is the Christ/God-figure, answers: "'Child,' said the Lion, 'I am telling you your story, not hers. No one is told any story but their own.'" This is the tension we rest into. We live lives full of love, care, and purpose. We pray for everyone on their journey, and we share our testimony of the goodness of God, but we will never truly *know* (as in fully experience) another person's story. We must all choose Christ individually. We do not control or save people.

This freeing truth was mixed with sadness, as I had to let go of my sense of control and learn to truly surrender and pray—not as a last resort but as my greatest act of love. Not to ensure a preconceived outcome but to simply love. We pray for friends to remember what we, too, have at times forgotten.

You are loved, and do not give up hope.

Take Action

Are there people in your life who are walking a path that isn't aligned with God's best? Are there those who need to know just how deeply loved they are? Take a moment to commit to daily prayer for these individuals. Release your need to control the situation, and trust that God's love is powerful enough to reach their hearts. Meditate on Psalm 33, particularly verses 12-22. He reached you, and He will not fail.

Prayer

Father, You know exactly where everyone is. I give You those who have hurt me and those I have hurt. I release the pain I still feel. I forgive those who have hurt me, whether intentionally or unintentionally. You are the Healer and Restorer. You are good.

"Let Your lovingkindness, O LORD , be upon us, According as we have hoped in You. For our heart rejoices in Him, Because we trust in His holy name. Our soul waits for the LORD ; He is our help and our shield. To deliver their soul from death And to keep them alive in famine. Behold, the eye of the LORD is on those who fear Him, On those who hope for His lovingkindness, A horse is a false hope for victory; Nor does it deliver anyone by its great strength. The king is not saved by a mighty army; A warrior is not delivered by great strength. He who fashions the hearts of them all, He who understands all their works. From His dwelling place He looks out On all the inhabitants of the earth, The LORD looks from heaven; He sees all the sons of men; Blessed is the nation whose God is the LORD, The people whom He has chosen for His own inheritance."

Psalms 33:12-22 NASB 1995

I Want a

I want a soft heart,

I want a heart that loves and feels,

I want a soft heart that is not hardened by the years,

I want a heart that never stops beating.

So take Your balm,

Massage the broken places,

I will not hide them anymore,

Take the places I do not understand

Take them in Your hand,

Massage the scars and give me,

A soft heart.

Soft Heart

The pain is great.

I want to run.

And sometimes I still hide.

Hiding works,

My heart grows hard.

And its beat is slowed by the walls that I am building.

But in my heart there is still Your gentle rhythm beating:

  "You, child, want

   A soft heart.

    You want

    A heart that loves

    And feels,

You want a heart not

hardened by the years."

And in *Your* hands, my *heart* never stops beating.

Growing up in the church, I witnessed many mistakes made by people I thought knew better. In my ignorance—probably mixed with a bit of pride—I assumed that being "Christian" meant being flawless. It didn't. Differences of opinions, offenses, betrayal, and a menagerie of vices threatened to poison my view of God and tempt me to grow bitter. After all the heart healing I had experienced though, I held a holy fear of becoming hard-hearted. The result was that I constantly prayed for a heart that remained tender and hopeful. It is not enough to have an emotional moment. In many seasons, we press in with awe and honor for WHO God is—a cold-blooded decision of the will.

> "The fear of the LORD is the beginning of wisdom, And the knowledge of the Holy One is understanding." Proverbs 9:10 NASB 1995

I had known enough love to know that distance from God was the greatest pain. I had lived that feeling-less, invisible life, and I didn't want to go back. I longed for the fresh breeze of childhood. I wanted to cling to the gifts of wonder, quick forgiveness, delight, hope, guileless honesty, freedom, and joy. As I stood on the precipice of adulthood I knew it would take more than idealistic dreams to finish this race well. I didn't *feel* childlike but I had tasted and seen something worth running towards.

The holy fear—the awe of God—is the beginning of the relationship. Not a trembling fear, too timid to approach but a longing wonder that brings us to the edge of glorious mountains and waits for eagle's wings. I was willing to fight and wait to know the *wisdom* of a childlike heart. This was Heaven on earth.

Take Action

There is a beautiful Japanese art form called kintsugi that takes broken shards of pottery and adheres them with gold. The result is a stunning, one-of-a-kind mosaic. In the artist's hands, broken things come to life. Jesus did not die to save us and present us as mended goods. Father God is a Master Artist.

Salvation means complete restoration. Picture your beating heart. Hold it in your hands, and offer it as a living sacrifice. Where hardness has settled in, ask God to massage it back to life. Then lean back into the love-filled rhythm of His heart beating.

The greatest evidence of healing is a willingness to trust God with what was once our greatest fear. Vulnerability takes intention. Let's give God our beating, childlike heart, and in return, He gives the kingdom of Heaven.

Prayer

Dear Jesus, You know me. You are acquainted with all my ways. You are fully capable of accomplishing everything that concerns me. I surrender the rejection, abandonment, fear, shame, anger, and self-hatred I feel. Please forgive me for believing those lies. I specifically surrender _____ (Name the person/s who hurt you) to You. I forgive them. Accomplish all that concerns them. Search and know them like You have searched and known me. Forgive them and bring them into freedom and the fullness of life. With Your artistry, transform our brokenness into something beautiful. In Jesus' name. Amen.

ANOTHER WORLD

A Conversation with Jesus

We stood at the edge of the woods today. Your
hand beckoned me to come.

"What is beyond the wood?" I ask. My question
once again mixed with fear.

"Beyond the wood?" You ask. Your hand slips
carefully into my own.

I look up.

Those eyes.
Always smiling, teasing, caring, inviting.
I lean my head on Your shoulder, our fingers
intertwined.

"Beyond the wood ..." You repeat with careful
wonder,

"Beyond the wood is another world."

The Journey

As I approached graduation, life was full of uncertainty. Another world awaited me—a world I could hardly imagine. I was still juggling three jobs, still unsure of what career I should pursue, and still feeling talentless. But I wasn't despairing. I understood that there would be no other time in my life when uncertainty could be so exhilarating. I was like an eagle perched high in the mountains. College could wait, and I could work. I had a small window of time to immerse myself in Jesus without the pressures of adulthood weighing me down.

I was keenly aware that the hours I devoted to Bible study, worship, and simply enjoying church services would become nearly impossible once I entered college, started dating, or had a family of my own. Another world was looming ahead of me, and I had a feeling I knew what that world was called: adulthood. So, I took a moment to look around the rooms of my heart and began packing my bags with a collection of giraffe and ballet pictures, daydreams and a sense of wonder. And, of course, forgiveness. I knew hurts would come; after all, as my dad told me in one of our bakery conversations that became so normal in later years—*it's impossible to love without experiencing some pain.*

Many times in my life, I have made a choice not to love. The idea of being "Invisible Lisa" has felt safer. Although the journey we are on is not safe, it is good. So here, on the brink of so much change, let's make a choice and embrace a new adventure. Be brave and allow your heart to imagine an adulthood that remains deeply *childlike.*

Take Action

Let's celebrate. Dream. Imagine. Make up a story. I love art, so painting is a beautiful outlet for me. The end product isn't as important as giving yourself permission to enjoy the process and get messy. Get lost on a walk with God. Use your imagination. Maybe pull out that blade of grass or small stone from the earlier devotional day and remember. There's nothing inherently special in the action or the objects themselves. Keep it simple. The power comes from choosing something today that restores the playful dreaming of childhood. *Pssst! You can't mess this up.*

Prayer

Father God, I choose the courage to embrace the season in front of me. Restore childlike faith in my heart and life. Let Your kingdom come and Your will be done, in me, and around me today. Amen.

Growing up

(Eighteen)
It happens without you knowing you know.
It happens without much thought.
You wake up and one day—
You've grown.—*Lisa 2002*

The Journey

I did it. I grew up. I couldn't stop it. I couldn't ride my big wheel singing "I don't want to grow up" forever—Some of you know what old-school commercial I'm talking about. By the time I turned 18, I was no longer afraid of growing up. I could look back and see how far I had come. I wasn't perfect, but it wasn't about being perfect. It was about love, and oh, how I had love. My Beloved had been faithful to me. As I looked into the future and wondered about romance, marriage, college, and the "real life" that would follow, I had no idea that I had been living "real life" all along. What I learned in those years, I have had to relearn over and over. Growing up—with jobs, college, the complexities of marriage, and family—brings plenty of opportunity for practice. These lessons have sustained me when despair, miscarriage, rejection, abandonment, and pain have come in waves that threatened to crush what little faith I had left. There has always been that undeniable spark of love. I have never been able to forget or reject the reality that Jesus' eyes of love on me.

Take Action

You've grown, too. You committed to a journey, and you are almost through—or rather, just beginning. The truths treasured today will transform tomorrow. The rest of your life starts today. Let today be the day that Love anchors your heart and you see the undeniable eyes of Love.

Take a moment to reflect on your journey. What memorable truths have impacted you along the way? Write down at least three lessons you've learned about love, forgiveness, or the beauty of being vulnerable. Think about the moments that shaped you and how these insights can guide you moving forward.

As you reflect, invite God into your thoughts. Thank Him for progress. Lastly, ask him to teach you to *dream again*.

As we stand at the edge of this journey together, I want to invite you to share your story. Just like threads in a tapestry, our experiences intertwine, creating something beautiful and unique. Your journey, with all its twists and turns, could inspire someone else on their own path. You never know how your words might weave into their lives, offering the strength and hope they need for the moment.

Pray with me the following poem.

Childlike

Happy Victory

Over land and over sea
Overcoming all of me.
Overwhelming love divine
Overcoming this heart of mine.
Heart rejoicing,
Heart at home.
My heart is singing as it roams.
Heart rejoicing heart at rest,
My heart is trusting you know best.

(*Graduation Song*, Lisa's Journal 2002)

"... I assure you and most solemnly say to you, unless you repent [that is, change your inner self—your old way of thinking, live changed lives] and become like children [trusting, humble, and forgiving], you will never enter the kingdom of heaven."
Matthew 18:3 AMP

Epilo

GLASS GIRAFFE AND GOLDEN SLIPPERS

I turned 18 today and graduated, too.

My mom gave me a chiseled glass giraffe—

delicate,

strong.

I love it.

Giraffes are my favorite animals.

Remember when I thought people could grow up to be

one?

Life is just beginning.

How can the journey have so much left to unfold?

I see an open road ahead and wonder—

What will the journey be like?

Will I make the right choices?

—grow lonely,

—or cold?

Another friend gave me a delicate golden ballet figure to

add to a necklace,

which I tied to a bit of rainbow-colored fabric. A little bit

of tapestry.

It shines—

golden, smooth, firm.

I run a finger over the precious gold.

Healing.

Dreams bloom in funny ways and funny places.
Your story doesn't run in straight lines, you know.
If it did, it wouldn't be much of a journey or story.

Who else would ever aspire to be a gleaming golden giraffe,
dancing ballet in too-tight tap shoes?
I smile.

I wiggle my bare feet into the rug. It is smooth and flat.
How wonderful the threads feel between my toes.
I giggle.

Somehow, on this day when I am supposed to be so grown up,
I feel very ...

Childlike.

"It is the glory of God to conceal a matter, but the glory of
kings is to search out a matter." — Proverbs 25:2 NKJV

"The beginning of wisdom is: Acquire wisdom;
And with all your acquiring, get understanding.
Prize her, and she will exalt you;
She will honor you if you embrace her." — Proverbs 4:7-8
NASB 1995

The Journey

I didn't know the adventure ahead of me. Courtship, marriage, motherhood ... growing up would come with all the joys and even the heartache I feared. But there was a well of relationship I could drink from and a worn spot on the rug where I could always sit. Remember, it is never a waste to spend it all on Him.

Take Action

Search out Love, and let Him find you in the most unexpected places. Allow your passion to bloom until you overflow.

Seek Him earnestly. In the quiet moments, when life feels mundane, and in the chaotic times that leave you breathless, remember: He is with you. In both the dark and the light, His love is a constant.

Do not forget your story. Embrace the adventures ahead. As you journey forward, let your heart remain open. Celebrate the victories, learn from the challenges, and share your story with others. You are part of a beautiful tapestry, one that reveals the artistry of a Creator Who delights in you.

The Prayer

So be it. Selah

About the Author & Design Artist

Lisa Douglass lives in upstate NY with her husband, 11 beautiful children, and a carousel of animals large and small. She loves the outdoors, saving money, and teaching others to garden in her spare time. This is her first book, and she has loved the journey of writing and learning graphic design. The art work was created using *Canva*.

Contributing Illustrators

Keira Douglass--*Contributed the beautiful Ballet Girl.*
An award-winning artist recognized at the New York State Fair, Keira has dedicated many years to the art of drawing, with a particular passion for the complexities of capturing the human form. Residing in upstate New York, she is currently pursuing a degree in business. In addition to her artistic endeavors, Keira enjoys a diverse range of interests, including soccer, cattle wrangling, writing, and art.

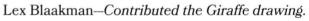

Lex Blaakman--*Contributed the Giraffe drawing.*
He is a Finger-Lakes-area artist with a versatile portfolio. His style is usually realistic, but sometimes abstract. His media is wood, canvas, and paper. His formats are deep relief woodcarving, in-the-round wood sculpture, acrylic paintings, graphite, and colored-pencil drawings. His subjects are people, animals and landscapes.
Lex sees art as a form of worshipping Jesus and letting God create healthy messages and prophetic signs through his hands. He believes that his art can be a catalyst for positive change by asking its audience to think deeper to gain understanding.

Acknowledgements

First and foremost, Jesus. My Heart.
Thank You. Thank You for knowing the words my heart wants to say.

To Keith, thank you for your tireless support, your patient listening, and for being a sounding board whenever I needed to talk things through. Your belief in me kept me going. Thank you for always thinking this was worth working on. I would like to extend my deepest gratitude to Valery Sykes and her Accelerated Author course and for the invaluable guidance and support throughout this journey. You helped turn a dream into a reality, and for that, I am eternally grateful.
To Courtney Rupe, my meticulous editor, thank you for your dedication to making this book the best it could be. Your thoroughness and keen eye have truly shaped this story. A special thank you to Gillian with Unlimited Design for your insightful suggestion and expert assistance with the graphic editing of this book. Your talent and wisdom about the publishing world pushed me over the finish line.
A heartfelt thank you to Keira, my most precious daughter. I want the second edition FILLED with your art. Thank you for the most precious drawing and for being an incredible reader and sounding board. Your creativity and support have meant the world to me. To Lex, for sharing your amazing talents. The giraffe is perfect!
I am also deeply grateful to Lisa, Pam, Cindy, Cathy, Bethany, Kacey, Joy, Anna, Lindsay, Aunt Nancy, and the countless others who have encouraged, prayed, and loved me—and this book—into being. Your kindness, faith, and support have lifted me up every step of the way. I love you all. Lastly, I know many more people deserve thanks. Thank you. Please know you are all in my heart, and your kindness has made the difference.

With all my love and gratitude,

Lisa D.

Coming Soon on

Amazon

Childlike Journal

The Journal for the Pursuit

By Lisa Douglass

Reflection & *Intention*

(Remember) ANYTHING YOU WANT TO REMEMBER- APPOINTMENTS TASKS EVENTS WORDS

Vision: _____

(Day): _____ (Month): _____ (Year): _____

Today's Truth in Focus	Goal of the Week

MUST DO

○ _____

○ _____

○ _____

CELEBRATE REFLECT

I AM SO GRATEFUL:

I WAS COURAGEOUS:

I MADE PROGRESS:

I WAS INTENTIONAL:

I SAID NO TO DISTRACTION:

Healthy Habit Tracker

Progress is the product of consistent movement. Keep track of what you do. When an area that regularly falls through the cracks, set a new INTENTION to make progress.

MOVEMENT ●   ● MAKE BED

JOURNAL ●   ● DEVOTION

PERSONAL GOAL ●   ● PERSONAL CARE

Believe Truth

Believe Truth

Made in United States
Troutdale, OR
12/10/2024

26258418R00071